LEARN FROM MY TRUTH

Poems of Inspiration

By:

Dana Grant

Copyright © 2016

To:

Mary and Sarah

February 4th, 2014

What have you done to deserve me?

To taste my soft lips,

Feel my round supple breast, to watch

My thighs and hips spread.

What have you done to deserve me?

I don't want your lust

I don't want your broken connection

I don't want your trial run.

What have you done to deserve me?

Dance

My ass rounded when I slid down that pole,

My body moving to the beat of my soul.

Music only I could hear, my breath perched

As I whisper 10 please.

See, most don't know that this is my release

This is my one chance to show all of my true beauty

And dance in circles around those who want me.

Security, no, you're not supposed to touch me.

Security, security, why can't anyone hear me?

When you're done you will join that long line

Of faceless men who misused me.

So many used and abused I can't fathom being true to just one.

I'm way too old to go crying to my momma

And to young for my life to be of meaning

So I would have bouts of crying and cutting, bleeding and cleaning.

Then I put on this mask of being normal,

While in my head I'm screaming,

"Something's wrong with me. Help. Me. I can't take no more!"

Then I met him, my creator, my Father, my King, and He said to me,

"Yes, this is your life, this is your journey and I was there carrying you

Through the roughest of times, now you will know me and love me

As I love you.

Colorado Springs

Sitting at a big oak table, slowly sipping peppermint tea,

gazing out of the kitchen window hearing the train go by is oddly comforting to me.

In the background I notice the white blanket mountains.

It's a beautiful, sunny morning and I don't have a care in the world.

I find myself full of energy I didn't know I had,

must be the West Coast or maybe the energy field that gives me

that serene feeling, like when I hike the mountains.

I belong here.

This. Feels. Like. Home.

Being a Queen/Quean

It excretes out of my pores,

Smells through my clothes like a soft scent of detergent.

It lives on the tip of my tongue

So that every word comes out with Grace.

You see it by the way that I walk and smile that I wear.

It hangs from the Ankh earrings I choose to wear

It makes my body taste like the exotic fruit I choose to eat.

It makes me glow as if I were carrying an extra soul.

I cannot hide it any longer.

Maybe I'm Selfish

Maybe I'm selfish.

I can't say I was ignorant.

I can't say I didn't know.

I knew exactly what I was doing to bring a child

Into this world, only to live like hell on Earth,

Then to die, and the death, the death possibly so

Horrendous it affects the actions and feelings of generations to come.

Wow!

Could that be why they say to mourn babies and celebrate the dead?

Could that be why mothers nowadays are ending little lives?

Instead of giving knowledge on how to survive?

Maybe I'm selfish, to give my body over for nine months,

To develop this strong love for another person when I don't even

Love myself.

Maybe I was thinking of self when I allowed this seed to get

So close to my womb that it entered and harvested a life,

Then to rip myself apart just trying to get him out.

Maybe, just maybe, I'm selfish.

Definition

Do not define me by my big, colorful words assuming that I am highly

intelligent.

Do not define me as my age, assuming wisdom follows.

Do not define me by my hair, or the veggie burgers I eat, as me being

Conscious.

Do not define me cause I bite my nails, assuming I can't handle

the higher source that flows through my fingertips.

Do not define me by name or the clothes that I wear.

Define me as a feeling you would get from an encounter.

Define me as a look into my soul thru my eye or the color of

My energy field.

Define me as my actions of care and intentions of love.

Define me as how much I give, or how naturally I take the

role of Mother Earth.

Define me without using words.

Define me as a simple musical note, or key.

Define me without a title or social status,

Or by how free my spirit is.

But….

Do not put me in your box or hold me to your rules,

For I can only be…Me.

Why I Wear My Ankh

To all who ask why I wear my Ankh

In hopes of one day taking my Ankh specter and inserting it

Into the ground to cause the biggest energy explosion

Letting any and every fall to the ground.

Oh, but when they awaken, when they rise, maybe this time they will begin

To think with the right side of their brain,

Making better decisions, raising better children.

Maybe the Earth will turn into the sun and each being will give

Off a golden yellow aura.

Maybe the sun will turn into the Moon, and the Moon will become

Just another planet.

Maybe, maybe each one will teach one

And there will be no child left behind.

Maybe we will experience life on different level?

Maybe the tall blades of grass will become outlets for us

To plug ourselves into and become one.

Are we not about love?

What is life without expression of higher self, like

Seeing a pretty flower, smelling its sweet scent,

And that putting a smile on our faces?

I'd rather die without expression, without love, without me having

Something to say cause it's long overdue and needs to be said.

I'm so tired of being quiet.

Daddy always said, "A closed mouth don't get fed," but somehow

I always ate or when gown folks talking....

You might get led by the pages of books they have read.

Connected

I wish to be connected again maybe.

One day maybe I will submit, or maybe you will surrender most beautiful thing, seeing that white flag waving.

Set aside problems; recognize the beauty within the both of us no one else seems to see.

How do I devour everything that's wrong and expect to be right once again?

I'm trying to blend, trying to be that carbon copy, comparing myself to these regular women, getting drunk to hide myself.

This is not me.

I am a sphere, a stone, the darkest, deepest dirt.

I am dying trying to hide my energy bringing true definition to savage.

Well, it's back to the square or better yet the same circle, no longer withdrawn through life's inner workings.

Once royalty, always dust off my crown, reposition it a top my head.

Just call me exotic.

I can only be me.

No matter whom comments, say good bye to my addictions, obsessions.

Polish up my aura and shine.

Spider Life

There's a spider that lives in my window.

I gaze out into the distance as he spins his web, allowing my future to look mystical.

The web sparkles like tiny crystals on my dreams.

Who is this spider? What's his name?

Why did he decide to spin his precious web on my window seal?

Maybe none of that matters.

He seems so small cause I've seen how large the land is and I've walked these streets and hiked these mountains.

I've taken this very moment and lived it realizing there could be a bigger picture, bigger than me.

What if I were a spider constantly spinning my web of life as my Creator lovingly watches, taking the time to teach me each of life's complicated lessons, guiding my web legs to be supported by the strongest beams?

What if he dismissed me like most do the spider?

What if he didn't care to know my name?

Lost Kings

I'm not at your neck I'm taking your head off, you dudes gonna make me bloody my pants, no menstrual.

Swell up my knuckles, no dimples

Making stacks of money your idol, it's so sinful.

You kings got so lost chasing different colors of pleasure can't find your way home with an address, map quest and directions.

Running in circles, popping out bundles of blessings, polo down book cover but nothing mental, you have to step out the box and live at an angle.

Learn, and then teach. Become a unit of luminance smells of red musk and sticky green, take away the confusion, make your kisses endearing.

Written on your arms I should see your life's story, on top of your head I should find your loc journey.

Feet so rough, stomping through the wilderness of North America,

Let me dig my petite fingers into your skin and massage away the looks of disgust. Use me to light up the faces of little girls, let them know what a queen consist of and I promise to fight and remain the definition of.

Some Days

Mama always said some days would be like today.

The sun isn't shining like it's the first day of snow, the ocean is calm and waves are too low.

Today feels like I'm standing in a long line and they ran out just as I reach the front.

I feel like not giving credit when it's due,

Or not speaking on the truth.

Today is foul, foul like having seeds planted in me, then getting sucked out like dust bunnies and flushed down the toilet.

Foul like getting unnecessary hysterectomies cause my doctor didn't feel like giving me options.

Or like the conspiracy to destroy queens, which are really women with dreams and knowledge of self.

I know the book cover to cover, but just can't pass the class.

The hardest lessons in life will take the longest time to learn.

I'm puking out the poisons of reality TV shows.

The image of me got flooded with those of the video vixens.

Today, there are no pretty flowers or pink rooms.

My struggles are not limited to acne and the cheerleading squad.

I wish today wasn't as real as a constant drinking to forget the pain, only for it to wear off and hurt like the first day of my menstrual, or a shot gun to my temple.

I'm fumbling; it's too many keys on this ring and I'm trying to unlock Heaven's gates,

Just to hear my mother say, some days would be like today.

Gifted

I'm still gonna speak in videos, shows and corner bookstores.

I am in every word, on every page in every book.

You can see me in every crack and crevice across the country.

You can find me in a stick on every tree in the back water towns of Pennsylvania,

Yet I am unrecognizable.

I changed so much that my DNA flees from my body in confusion

Like the blue blood that flows thru my veins and turns red when it

Reaches oxygen which is "O",

And that's cold like liquid nitrogen which is LN2,

Or like H2O when it leaks between my fingers no matter how tight I hold my hand.

You see this time I let him enter without precautions,

Without the proper planning, then was ridiculed by the poor performance.

This was a walking plague, spreading and touching every aspect of my life.

Call me a scapegoat, better yet ground zero, the beginning of the end,

Quarantined to this Midwest comfort zone.

I'm not your 9 to 5 working, Starbucks drinking, button down wearing,

Straight hair rocking size 3, wanting to be anybody but myself zombie.

The words that I spit are not scripted.

I'm. Just. Gifted.

Who Am I…Nobody!

Who am I? Nobody.

The question is who are you? Where do you stand?

Don't listen when I hold out my hand,

I have no choice but to stand right off the freeway with a sign that says, I will work for food.

Look over me; pass me, thru me, but never directly at me.

Get out a pad and pen and write me off.

Throw a rug on my back; leave your footprints on my arms, curse me to my face.

Dropped out early, 4 kids, no home, no car, bad credit, no loans, falling for any ounce of kindness than feeling that thin blade dagger pierce my skin.

Guess that wasn't a real friend or potential spouse.

One day I will be pretty enough to see, or even have pretty seeds, the kind that don't begin with forced tears.

I am more than soundless screams and silent nights, unspoken fears talking at me like they do children and all I have left is my dreams, to be the biggest and baddest in the land,

The loudest voice with a plan,

Then reality sets in and again, who am I…Nobody.

The real question is, who are you?

Where do you stand?

Cycle

I drove a nail thru your painting.

Thought I was going to hang it. Hole punched the side to place in a binder.

Think I'm going to set this one out, (the painting that is.)

I refuse to believe you've grown in 30 days,

I refuse to believe you have brand new ways.

The stakes of becoming your wife is deadly.

If it wasn't the many abortions that I would go thru after you convinced me and promised to be by my side, only to come back later and say you never held a gun to my head,

Then surely what would take me out is choosing to believe the bogus receipt you brought home from the clinic down the street.

Ignoring the look the doctor gave every time she sat to write the prescription, promising to never let you disgrace me again.

I waited for the day that I may want children again.

I waited for our love to become more than your pretty picture.

I waited for you to beg me to come home again.

I let you in, after the cycle spins and again it's,

Wash. Dry. Repeat.

Don't Complain

I couldn't stay away. The key to the secret garden was burning a hole in my pocket,

I walked past.

Death kindly tipped his hat to me as if I were a Southern belle,

then came for me in the night like robbers and thieves entered my subconscious and compelled me to confess.

Yes, I spiked your drink with the ability to heal,

Gave etiquette lessons for Queens,

Baked you a cake laced with chaparral root,

Cleaned your copper with vinegar,

Tuned your crystals to positive,

White saged your living space,

Assembled your alter,

Placed crystals in the North, South, East, West,

Packed your sacred wombs with clay, lifted your head,

Straightened your back, aligned you with the Most High,

Raised your prince from the dead twice,

Gave shape to the woman of your dreams.

Got rid of low level energies,

Kept you on your square, cleared your third eye,

Helped you to understand that you are the original Asiatic Black Man.

Cooked vegan food, gave your body a chance to heal itself

Replaced your zinc after we laid and you came,

Washed and retwisted your locs,

Gave you the Game, sheltered you from the rain,

And, NEVER ONCE DID I COMPLAIN!

Our Love

Chased him away to some other race,

I would love to blame him, the truth is,

If I was everything he needed then he wouldn't have went looking,

Or maybe he just wanted assorted flavors, a variety pack,

Maybe the subliminal message he learned in elementary was

That of the forbidden fruit,

Maybe he sat for a rotted, bitter piece then decided to roll with

Me.

Well then you will receive sweet whispers in the form of text.

For the remainder of the evening you stroked my ego, wasn't

Afraid to give PDA's, fed my soul with your wallet, and announced me as

Your mate.

So if my heart was your dick it would be pumping outside of my chest, holding

An erection on top of my breast,

Swing those long locs ferocious lion; pounce on me like its suppertime,

And I am warm meat. Enter my realm where nothing exist

But red skies and thick thighs.

I love you because in this world so many don't know they are, but you do.

One late night you hopped out of your comfort zone

And took a chance, you opened your soul to me,

You saw the beautiful rose past the thorns,

You saw the light beacon, responded to the SOS,

With 911 you gave me the key that I may unlock the door,

Open it, walk thru, raise all the windows and air out the house;

You are my stability, the fixer of all my problems,

You hold me all night when most give up every time.

You quench your thirst, you think of me first.

You have the gentlest touch, even when mad,

I love you because your name is written on my soul

And forever our story will be told.

If there ever comes a day you choose to deny our love,

Well I hope to be reunited with my ancestors.

I hope that my precious vessel turns to dust.

You see, a day without you is a simple hanging, a week,

A messy butcher of my ingredients, so please, sentence me

To a lifetime of bondage;

Drown me in your bodily fluids.

Cleveland

Having the knowledge on how to drive at the age of 12,

Doing 80 in a snow storm, we petty, flying down a one way residential,

Just call us ready.

When the lights are red, but you can ignore that shit on the late night trip.

No tourist, we are the road less traveled.

We got coats for the cold winter, not the rain,

our reactions you cannot tame.

We are the town of the most talented, where everybody's a rapper

and still remain the underdogs, underground,

just ask the Dawg Pound.

Home of the flyest fits and homemade hits,

the critically underestimated, the over thinkers,

most hair popped and nails rocked coming down in old schools

for the summer and selling them shits when the leaves fall.

Where the city girls pick cantaloupe, but still walking barefoot

to the ground, home of the Moorish science temple

and the O. E. S., home of the legendary Westside market,

fearless hearts of courageous lions roam these streets.

They call me Bae Root after the jungle where I was born

And raised.

My. City.

We stuff big words into small sentences,

bend them up like magicians, we don't have competition,

We're first, second and third. We stay fresh like the 574's

Or 54.11's, classic, like the black and white movies,

Arsenic and Old Lace. We got a love that just runs rampant,

wild, biting anything that's warm blooded.

We headliners, and anywhere else is the fourth spot,

from the Top.

Black Woman's America

Painted red lips cover the blood slits

Wash the fermented milk off our breast, feed the leaves on the trees,

Bring cure to the diseased after the storm destroys,

Seeing is everything, but sometimes perception lies or hopes of misunderstandings,

My sight is my truth, yours not a prob, it's the fabric in your DNA

so different, yet we cut from the same.

I'm closer that I think to chilling on the black beach

with black water and black sand cause everything,

Black is beautiful.

Your eyes chose sleep cause it's the cousin of death.

If that's so then who is your Creator and why did they choose me?

If you sift thru my dirt you will find a big butt brown sista

with the markings of a slave, before that was a loc rocking

Queen from Morocco.

We are the absolute most hated ever since we started creating.

White men want to rape us. Sara Bartman.

Black men wants to degrade us, Video Vixens,

Then trade us for some other race and label her queen and we still trying to fight

for that house nigga spot, blonde weave blue contacts

while they plump up their lips and put implants in their hips

and stole our spot.

Burn up that brown paper bag, our crowns we must retrieve.

It's not gone, it just needs Fix-a-Flat, you know that stuff them girls

was shooting in their butts, letting other misguides speak for them

on the mainstream rap records,

silently dying in hotel rooms and storage units,

leaving our young girls to figure out why no legacy becoming

disfigured from behind.

Let us rewind this wrong and make it opposite of left,

We been too busy playing checkers, not chess.

Room

Featured in book, <u>Hessler Poetry Anthology 2015</u>

    I didn't mean to lead you into an empty room. You see, that room was once filled with dreams and magic pixie dust. I'm sorry I pushed you in and you had no choice but to walk across the broken shards of hope. I expected you to run away, but I forgot your feet were bleeding too much.

    I left you there to see the broken parts of me, like the bloody panties of my rape at 15, and the knife I used to cut my wrist. I apologize for walking out and looking back at you as if you were already the past, and I'm sorry that I locked your heart in this room, swallowed the key knowing that I would never return. I'm sorry that I wasn't free for you. I apologize for presenting myself to you with bruised wrists and cut off feet. I wanted so much to see past the long talks and I'm holding on for dear life to the truth and reality, so I had to leave.

    I'm sorry I left an implied noose in that room. You see, I expected it to burn along with those tragic memories. I do remember the good times. I remember the love tripping over my untied shoes. I race back there, spit up the key, oh wait, I already forgot I have no feet. I open the door only to find an empty room, once filled with dreams and magic pixie dust.

Scorn

Maybe she's scorned from the last opposite that left his shirt in her closet.

Maybe it's darkness until she closes her eyes, like a witch, she hops on that white stick and prays that the nicotine takes her away.

Maybe she'll take that apology and use it to sweep up that broken glass that reflects her tears.

I'm talking to the person that lives in the pupil of a single eye, the one that hangs from the fourth rib,

Somewhere down the line you being a grown man became a lie, and she couldn't see those warning signs with a naked eye.

Now every day is about where you lay. She stalks and follows the trail of broken hearts and bread crumb, paved road, open path that your ancestors left behind.

She ran until she got hit with that stray. Who's to say that bullet had her name?

It was wrapped with a red rose, hollow tip before point of impact.

Her promise, the next one that enters her thighs will definitely deserve to be there.

No more lowered standards.

Settling is not an option for survival sake,

The love can't be real if the flowers are fake!

ANNOUNCEMENT

ATTENTION, ATTENTION, ATTENTION

ALL GERMS, VIRUSES, DISEASES AND DEMONS…

YOUR DAYS OF WREAKING HAVOC ARE OVER!

YOU ARE NO LONGER WELCOME HERE,

THE PURIFICATION PROCESS WILL NOW BEGIN.

WE WILLSTART OFF WITH STARVING YOU FROM THE POISONS AND GARBAGE THAT YOU LOVE SO MUCH,

THEN YOU WILL BECOME VERY WEAK, SICK, AND SHRINK, FOLLOWED

BY DETERIORATION AND DECAPITATION....

FINALLY, A DISAPPEARANCE.

I CAN'T PROMISE IT WILL BE PAINLESS.

THANK YOU.

This has been an announcement brought to you by better health, S. O. S. (Saving Our Souls).

Commencing body cleanse in 5....4....3...2....1

Liberated Wombman Day

Let's make our day Liberated Woman Day, one that Hallmark doesn't taint, no packed lunches.

No we didn't construct the buildings but guess what? We run the town.

Take your arranged marriage and shove it where the sun don't shine! Modern day slavery sold to the highest bidder.

Wanna speak on Michelle Knight situation, but you couldn't possibly walk 10 years in her shoes and you were probably gonna get me a 6 dollar birthday card too along with the bathroom candle and the pissed in lemonade.

I did the knowledge back in '03 which really makes sense cause my born day is 126, but I was mentally freed on 621 and I live in 216, so anyway you add it equals 9.

I count up the square mileage in my state, in my city and even these couple of two by fours lined up on my floor,

It doesn't add up! We are so disconnected and that's all we've ever experienced. How could we miss the united way? Let us find out on this day.

Let us burn in our heads the memories of those who paved the way, the idea that got us to that Underground Railroad and the want for a better life that outweighed the fears.

So sign my name to that petition Jessica Care Moore, and it is long overdue T. Miller. To all the wombs in the world………..

HAPPY LIBERATED WOMBMAN DAY!

KKK

How did this KKK member get into my bedroom? The most sacred of places, the most peaceful place.

Why is he standing here cowardly, dressed in bed sheets, hiding, smelling like a roasted pig, looking at me with disgust and judgment, yelling his racial slurs so loud it's wakening my neighbors?

Hating me so much his eyes turned red. I'm looking to pull the fire alarm.

I want to run but my children are asleep in the very next room.

How sick is your mind to think the worst thing you can do is forcefully push yourself inside of me until my screams become tears and until my tears become silence, then squeeze my neck until I've taken my last

breath and string my naked body up as a lesson to the rest?

My Love

Every man that I've ever laid with has fallen in love with me.

I'm cursed because I don't know how not to make love to their souls.

I gently caress the very core of these men,

I listen to their deepest darkest secrets.

I tell them I'm their property to hold and to have at any given day, any given moment.

I make them feel they're safe in me.

I put their mind and body at ease.

I recognize how heavy the world weighs on their shoulders, and I massage away the pain.

I make them close their eyes and take them by the hand, lead them to a peaceful, heavenly place.

All it takes is one look into my eyes to see their future.

One touch of my hand sets their skin ablaze,

One sniff of my natural skin fragrance, one taste of my sugary soft lips and they can't resist,

One sound of my voice makes them choose me every time to share their lives, teach their daughters to be just like me, and love their sons,

They always fit me so perfectly into their little lives, the problem is,

They never fit into mine.

How Much

I want to kill him and that's how much I love him.

I want to be the last person he sees and I want to squeeze until he can't breathe.

I want to be the reason for the last tears he cries.

I want to be the face on the back of his eye lids,

I want to sharply roll over on him, softly piercing the inner casings of his heart and be the last to kiss his lips until I taste red.

I want to open his mouth, cut out his tongue just so he can't apologize for what's to come.

I want to be the last person he hears whispering sweet nothings in his ear,

"Everything's going to be okay."

I want to sit and hold his hand until his soul is forced to a far away land.

I want to sprinkle his burned ashes along the sand, and I will miss him when he is…Gone.

Dear No Name

Dear No Name,

     I stare at a picture of you every night before I go to bed, asking God why he made you so attractive, why it was so comforting to hear your voice, why I laugh hysterically at your corny jokes. Why your walk is the best thing I've seen in my life and these eyes witnessed a million man march and why you so desperately want to walk those streets alone. Why I want to keep you under lock and key, like a diamond encrusted crown or a million dollar painting, or why every time you kiss my lips it's so soft and gentle, yet everything about you has always been rough. Why your hands are so strong, or why upon first insertion my body starts to seize until it's left in a pool of sweat, like you were the problem and the only answer.

Your one year of being in a relationship is like a regular man's ten and your one discretion is like accidentally knocking over a glass of warm milk and you're tired now. All those marathons you ran from, bed to bed, jumping hurdles of needy women ignoring all their suitcases from past relations, beating up their brothers for caring too much, talking all the shit and not giving a fuck.

Rest now and make sure no one is there to slice you up.

Mother Earth

Blocking this artificial sun cause it gives off nothing and it makes my 3rd eye want to cry,

The time when my subconscious thrives I'm supposed to be earthing but my feet can't reach the ground for all the asphalt pushed around.

I fell asleep with my cell phone by my head,

Awake to ashes of brain cells that burned away during the night, each organ attempted to detox itself

But looked around at all the fast food sludge and processed cheese

And decided not to.

My body shut down.

My soul levitated to another realm to get away from the rotting smell of my midnight snack.

My waste not sliding out my bladder, not trickling down, wishing I could yell in one ear and cover the other so you could hear…

This is important…

Chant my words backwards so it becomes a spell,

Shower you in my spit cause every drop is knowledge and my juices start civilizations, even my feces organically fertilizes.

I'm barefoot to the ground.

Vines travel up my legs and hang on for dear life, begging me not to disconnect.

Sounds of the late night wind whispers my name. I am Mother Earth.

America #2

America is a tall, colonial, Caucasian with a Cherokee hat and blood stained hands, his stars and striped pants stink of deflowering juice. America in the flesh.

I'm wishing there was an opt out button for society, lie, cheat, murder to get to the top of the barrel, forcing more mothers to get registered pistols, trying to give the king back what we think is the modern day tool to protect.

Little black boy, your mother is fighting for you even when you don't listen, even when your teddy bear is missing. No peace. Our minds at its best when it's total chaos all around, when objects burst into flames and when we're afraid to turn out all the lights at bedtime, when love and pain has the same scream, so don't put us in the woods with the croaking frogs and the rivers and streams.

We need gunshots and screeching tires and loud sirens. We need to be where the mothers are crying and where you can smell the burning bodies. Our past is too ugly to put on paper, to gory to spread across listening ears like an urban legend blowing breath on the pages, giving life to these poems.

We need transfusions. It took too much melanated skin, but some birds aren't supposed to be caged. You see, their backs were made too strong and their wings soar like the true definition of freedom and their bodies are filled with colors so bright it could have only come from pain and struggle.

Their minds have too many ideas for their bodies to sit still and their souls sing the sweetest melodies and they shine brighter than the full moon at midnight,

So, you little black boy, this poem is for you. You are more than this wake up.

You are a king.

America

If I lay for America that bitch will hold me down throw a pillow over my face and the only way to get her off is to roll over and play dead, then hope that my bravery doesn't go unsaid, and hope that my body isn't full of lead, and hope that my locs aren't just called dreads.

When she comes for me I will not go quietly into the night. I won't go down without a fight. Mary taught me that now you want me to bend and take it up the back, you want to raise my children to be called black, you want to raise them to believe your lies of history and plant grenades in their spines so they forget their strong back and emasculate them, make them weak wrist.

I equipped my sons with rifles of knowledge.
My daughters with semi automatics for
wisdom and I overstand, and we even keep a
couple of them hollow tips for the KKK,
cause we're not scared and we don't play.

You Gay

You gay, but not a supporter. You, I sing this in my song but don't really live that life gay. You popcorn gay, you gay but nobody really knows when the lights are out and the doors are closed.

The day that black women died from bad butt injections, guess your mic was in the off position.

Where you from island girl? Yea you hollered that when you came out, but you not reppin so where you really from? What's her story, did you take for your own?

You want us to believe you crawled from a rock, and then you claim to be the one from the five Burroughs where the queens are constructed, the knowledge factory.

How dare you not address your race! You're a coward, just like a sedative and rape and just like Barbie. Your crowned accessories are fake but you talk more about being gay, having hair weave and butt injections more than your real name, Onicka.

We waited for you to come out Barbie and you let us down, Tylenol PM, bet you can't sleep at night. Bet you got a headache. Bet your weave too tight.

Mattel had a recall, so follow that line right back. The only reason you are followed is cause you, like us, lost and confused. You taught us that we don't shine as bright unless there's a pink weave glued to our scalp and our walk isn't tough unless there are two water balloons shaking in our butts.

And even if you have one naturally it's okay to constantly shake and show off in the most inappropriate places, like work and church. And stop writing songs for our lost daughters to do nothing but twerk to.

Black Box

They called me black as if I were dipped in tar, colored filled as if somehow Crayola made me in his image. Since you want me to possess this let me spit you a rainbow of black and blue stories and how black forever became associated with strange fruit and hooded men and because of their jealousy soon poured red, and our souls levitated from the green grass into the gray skies, and while you hid and burned, the sun poured yellow rays into our crowns and just like the crayon box, we come in all different shades. Truth is no one is pure. You can go ask your grandma for that fact. You see, the devil made you a diseased soulless coward. You clear, you don't deserve to be in the same box as me. I'm Asiatic earth and not to be classified as black. And I won't check the box that best describes my race, you couldn't possibly understand how complex my melanin flows, I'm in tune with the way the wind blows and how tall the trees grow. Therefore, I can never fit, nor will I ever be found in your little black box.

Ungrateful

When faced with reality you ran, and that became a common characteristic.

Being dense, you wanted straight, long hair with light skin and along with that exotic.

You got poverty; you got no goals, no dreams, education, never going past a lap dance.

You got confused children, steady trying to figure out where to fit in. You try to feed them knowledge as if their tiny brain can hold the Moroccan dynasty era.

Your seeds were planted in useless soil, land of no harvest, and success will only meet you like the lottery. One in over a million, or cuando las ranas crein pelo, when frogs grow hair.

You're death and destruction.

You traded grass for concrete. You let a voodoo priest enter your circle and spit pig's blood in your face. You're a disgrace.

You eat off the backs of hard working single mothers.

You're dishonorable.

You shake hands with no eye contact. You don't know what it means to be a man of your word.

You're sneaky. You keep secrets like a rapist. You're hateful, but it all started with the man in the mirror.

You're ungrateful cause you just can't fix your mouth to say, Thank You.

The Devil

The devil came in with me, now he's been here since Adam and Eve.

Since the days of the garden with that tempting apple tree and the talking bush that lost its leaves. He is now located near your left sleeve, sitting on your shoulder, whispering about deception and greed.

I am defeated by a little boy who swears he's a grown man, promises to be more important than Martin, Malcolm and the President.

Guess you're not pulling up a chair to that humble pie anymore. You probably still eating with your tongue split in two still got that plug up your nose and suds behind your ears.

Made a contract agreeing to give 100% around you when I'm not, it's however much I choose. You can't seem to shake that sweet taste that had you hooked since and early age of 14. Street life, much like that night I watched over you while you slept cause you had to swallow your stash.

You call me your queen but you can't answer the phone around me. I run. I hate me for keeping fake ass niggas in my circle, in the sense of smiling in my face and tell another the same.

It's cool. You wanna play the game, but my jerseys are on the wall. You got straight legs and feet but still wanna crawl. Tighten up, they watching my finger just like they watch the ball.

Don't see that ring, the plans go into action, they trying to invest in the happily ever after. I'm laughing. You trying to sell the same dream you sold 12 years ago.

Gone

You, not properly caring for your womb

you fish, and it probably came from that married man you been laying with,

knowing he not divorcing his wife, choosing to believe you're the love of his life,

Not seeing him with those pointy ears and long red tail.

You lazy.

All it takes is to open your eyes you sideline subway, you get no passes.

You aspire to be in someone else's shoes. You think the answers to all your problems is a winning lottery ticket or between the sheets of a successful man's bed.

You make up 85% of the walking dead.

Your face is next to the definition of ignorance. I guess setties got wife dreams too though you carry the price of pleasure in your Louis Vuitton bag. The road to hell is paved with tight jeans and blonde weaves.

And you're treating me like I'm the treacherous whore in your nightmares?

I'm Asiatic earth and only time can tell if you will ever reach the top shelf.

Although I'm standing in my own imperfections and I've spent time that wasn't always productive.

My chakra is not on your energy chart, and just like the rose I left on my ancestor's grave,

You too will be here today, gone tomorrow.

He Is Love

He is my best friend,

My first real kiss,

Yet, my last chance.

He is the color orange, bright, upbeat, always positive.

My protector.

6'2", mysterious, weird, and handsome.

Hard worker by day, bookworm, by night, hustler.

He never sleeps; he carries my passion neatly folded in his wallet next to his strength.

He blankets me with warm rose petals,

he walks miles in his size 12's just to get a glimpse of my face.

He is freedom and free to hold my hand if every he felt erased.

He stands on love and that is more concrete than concrete

with steel rods and beams.

You see, I found him in my dreams and somehow that dream must have manifested into reality, cause here he is walking toward me with a bright, white smile and glowing brown skin.

And if ever intelligence had a look with the mind as complex as the inner workings of a Grandfather's clock,

even though I turned my back and wrote him off like Maggie's little sister,

this moment is what separates the men from the boys.

I pretend he asks for my hand and promises to wed.

We'd swim through grief and pain just to connect,

he being so real I got no choice but to submit.

He. Is. Love.

Learn From My Truth,

Sincerely,

    Dana Grant

www.ingramcontent.com/pod-product-compliance
Lightning Source LLC
Chambersburg PA
CBHW031419040426
42444CB00005B/642